GOD'S Lady

**BECOMING A
WOMAN OF GOD'S DESIGN
THROUGH SOUL-CARE**

AUGUSTA M. REED

Bible quotations and references were taken from THE AMERICAN STANDARD BIBLE, Copyright 1960 by the Lockman Foundation. Used by permission. All rights reserved.

Bible quotations and references were taken from THE AMPLIFIED BIBLE, Copyright 2015 by the Lockman Foundation. Used by permission. All rights reserved.

All other Bible quotations and references were taken from THE KINGS JAMES BIBLE. Public Domain.

Cover Design: Alicia Redmond www.aliciaredmondministries.com

Editor and Interior Design: Deborah A. Gaston www.deborahgaston.com

ISBN (Paperback) 979-8-9864241-2-5

ISBN (E-book) 979-8-9864241-3-2

What women are saying about *GOD'S LADY: Becoming a Woman of God's Design through Soul-Care*

This book eloquently emphasizes the qualities of the *chayil* woman, portraying her as a multifaceted and godly individual. The author effectively addresses issues relative to the importance of self-worth, relationships, and societal challenges while offering practical wisdom. This book is a comprehensive and insightful exploration of the Proverbs 31 woman. It emphasizes her grace, dignity, and godliness while highlighting that her true beauty is manifested through the qualities of her soul and spirit. The author encourages women to recognize their value in God's eyes and advocates for healthy relationships, emphasizing the importance of prioritizing God and maintaining one's individuality.

Candace Reed, Professional Makeup Artist–Candy Coated Faces Makeup, Cincinnati, Ohio

When so many are focusing on things that are happening in the world, this book is right on time. This book will help us remember where our focus should be, which is on our Lord and Savior, Jesus Christ. I appreciate how Augusta is transparent about some of the things she has been through and her example for those who may be going through, too. She lets them know they can make it if they trust God and let Him be their key focus. I have been so encouraged by this book.

Minister Mary Givens, Nashville, Tennessee

This anointed book gives modern-day insight into how the *chayil* woman is mysterious yet so complex that she can't be duplicated. It also tells women that becoming complete (God's lady) is not determined by assets, notoriety, or beauty but by obedience to God through the Holy Spirit. The model of a virtuous woman was defined by a woman and given as an example for a king. Precious jewels (ladies) of all ages can use this model to be Kingdom-minded chayil citizens in a culture that says differently.

Mrs. Hertia A. Mims, Visionary Specialist and Life Coach at The Mims Company, Dayton, Ohio

If you're a lady looking for encouragement, this book is it. Reed reminds us of the value we have in Christ as women, which we sometimes forget. Discover what it means to be an incredible woman through God's lens. Filled with biblical truths, this book will enlighten women on the true definition of beauty as one of God's ladies. A truly special message to all women from any walk of life. Read and be encouraged!

Shalena Forde, Educator, Worship Leader, Cincinnati, Ohio

GOD'S LADY: Becoming a Woman of God's Design through Soul-Care displays the value of true womanhood! It describes how the *chayil* woman (Proverbs 31 woman) displays radiant inner beauty and industriousness and supports her husband, family, and community. This book describes how this woman exudes valor: possessing God-given strength and dignity to face any challenge. What's most fascinating is that she is dear to the heart of God —someone to admire! Becoming God's lady is attainable as we continue to yield to the guidance of the Holy Spirit.

Calandra Rivers, Educator, Savannah, Georgia.

GOD'S LADY: Becoming a Woman of God's Design through Soul-Care gives women of all ages a good look into how we should carry ourselves and how we should see ourselves as women of God. It makes us examine our inward woman. The book tells single women about the type of men we should ask God for and the qualities to look for in a godly man. Also, this book gives insight to women over 60 on how their lives aren't over, regardless of whether they are married, widowed, divorced, or single. I highly recommend this book. It will bless your soul and encourage you no matter what stage of life you are in.

Elder Tamra J. Thornton, Sunday School Superintendent, Greater Grace Temple, Springfield, Ohio

This book had me in tears. I couldn't put it down. The information in the book about rubies impacted me in a significant way, causing me to realize that everything about me is God-given and every aspect of my personality was placed inside me from my mother's womb. The book's message spoke straight to the heart of spiritual abuse and the level of cruelty displayed to keep victims trapped in self-doubt with little or no confidence to move forward. However, the book also states that the victim's only option is moving forward in Jesus' name. The chapter that discussed bucking the system and being a hurt-mate, not a help-mate, caused me to call my husband and repent for not honoring him in the spirit of submission on every level.

Minister Ann Marie James, Th.B., M.Min., Chaplain, Savannah, Georgia

It is refreshing to know that much like the ruby, even with all my imperfections, it is the failures and flaws of my life that make me and my story rare—one to be treasured and incomparable to anyone else's. It's also empowering to see how even the most painful parts of my journey can have redeeming qualities, and God can and will use my unique testimony to speak life over those around me. This book helped me see that God isn't looking for flawless, polished women with no substance to be world changers but for those whose beauty, rarity, and value come from some of life's most pressing and painful blows. I was pleasantly surprised when the two Josephs were so beautifully and thoroughly explained in what I thought was just a book about and for women. Augusta not only took great care to share how these two men walked out their destinies with integrity and determination but also showed how these two men of the Bible set the bar for what a man of God and of honor should look like. The book shows readers that royalty begets royalty, and for women to walk in their God-given rights as daughters of the King, each must seek the qualities of a king for a man in her life.

Kelly Letner, Worship Pastor-Eagle Rock Church, Pickerington, Ohio

Contents

Acknowledgments

Jesus Christ never ceases to amaze me. He has gifted me with the ability to fluidly transfer my thoughts into written words. I never dreamed of writing books, let alone this seventh one. My goal for each book is that He will be glorified and readers edified.

I want to dedicate this book to the "early" Bishop Thomas "Darron" Jordan. Darron was my dear friend who supported every facet of my ministry from day one. He and his precious wife, Jacquelyne, gave me my first opportunity to be the keynote speaker for their church's first women's conference in 1995, soon after the release of the original edition of **GOD'S LADY**. That opportunity repeated itself for twenty wonderful years. There has to be a spark to ignite a fire. That first conference was the spark that ignited my national conference-speaking ministry. Bishop Jordan "went home to rest and reward" days after I began to pen this book. I know if he were alive, he would buy and endorse this book, as he did each of my previous ones. I cannot thank God enough for his and Jacquelyne's friendship and support.

I dedicate this book to the many women who have made indelible impressions on my life. These women represent a multiplicity of ethnicities, cultures, ages, and life experiences. Some taught me "what not to do," while others demonstrated the poise, power, and positive influence I believe every female follower of Christ should exemplify. Through the wisdom of the Holy Spirit, I have learned to appreciate them all.

Ladies over 60, I dedicate this book to you. Your life may have dramatically changed over the past few years. Significant chapters of your life may have ended. However, those were chapters, not the entirety of your story. May the words of this book empower you to add new and exciting chapters to your unique narrative. I pray that this book will cause you to rediscover your "fire" so you can continue exploring, growing, and excelling in everything you do. God has given you life, so LIVE!

To those ladies in their "middle season" ...

Your plethora of responsibilities causes you to be constantly pulled in multiple directions. As you care for everyone and everything, don't forget to care for yourself. May the contents of this book energize your soul and rejuvenate your spirit.

This book is also dedicated to the younger generation (teens and young adults). As you read this book, allow God to endow you with His wisdom and knowledge. The world may call you Generation Z, but you were not created to bring up the rear in society or God's Kingdom. May you discover "all" of who you were created to be. Jesus expects you to learn, accomplish, and contribute more than your predecessors. Be courageous. Be confident. Be outstanding.

Remember:
"Every lady is a woman, but every woman is not a lady!

~GOD'S LADY, The Complete Woman

How It All Began

A while ago, a video was shown at a Christian women's gathering that was supposed to show examples of exemplary women in various facets of society. Indeed, the women displayed were considered high achievers in sports, entertainment, and politics. However, during their many speeches and interviews, I never heard 80% of them mention a personal relationship or belief in Jesus. To top it off, many of their personal lives were publicly messy and chaotic, to say the least. I wondered why the conference presenters thought of them as role models. The Scripture that immediately came to mind was Mark 8.36: *"For what shall it profit a man if he shall gain the whole world, and lose his own soul?"*

I envisioned these women transitioning into eternity without their popularity and prestige. I could see them standing before Jesus with no applause from crowds of admirers. I pictured them at the throne of God with nothing of eternal value to present to Him. Instead of being motivated, I was saddened.

That incident caused me to realize the necessity for me to do more to educate and empower women in ways that would heighten their strengths and address their needs from a comprehensive perspective—with Jesus as the focal point and the Bible as the foundation.

In 1995, I penned my first book, **GOD'S LADY, *The Complete Woman*.** Prior to that, the only lengthy documents I had ever written were diagnostic reports in my role as a Speech-Language Pathologist. I was committed to completing this God-given assignment. Remember, this was before the days of email, the Internet, digital documents, and online publishing. Everything was done through phone calls and snail mail.

I vividly recall the details of that process. I was working full-time, had a husband and two young children. In addition, we were all involved in our community and church. I did most of my writing late at night when everyone was asleep. Keeping those hours was arduous since I had never been a night owl. Each time I sat at my word processor (google it), the words were supplied by the Holy Spirit. It took me nine months to write the manuscript and four months to get it published and ready for the public.

Because I didn't know any authors and didn't have practical information readily available, I dealt with rip-offs and rejections from literary agents and publishers. I finally found a reputable self-publishing company that would do everything I needed. It was costly but worth every penny.

After I had the book in hand, I thought I had endured the most challenging part of being an unknown author. Little did I know that marketing would be a prominent and continual obstacle. I was shocked to experience the dishonesty of major Christian bookstores. They said they would display and sell my book, but instead, they hid it in storage rooms or threw it into the trash.

Nevertheless, several "Mom and Pop" bookstores graciously allowed me to have book signing events and sold the book for several years. Although that era has passed, and those stores no longer exist, I am forever grateful for their encouragement and help.

A few years after **GOD'S LADY** was published, I gave a copy to a visiting pastor. To my surprise, he called me the following week and ordered 200 books, which he gave to the women of his congregation. That support took the sting out of the previous negative experiences and proved that my small book would make a big impact.

Because I was "unknown," which limited my marketing sphere,

I sought the Lord about how to get this book into the hands of those who needed it. He answered my prayers by connecting me with prison ministries that allowed me to use **GOD'S LADY** as a seminar manual. **GOD'S LADY** was used consistently for over nine years in the largest female prison in Ohio. It was also used in a men's facility as the manual for their marriage empowerment groups. These groups were comprised of male residents and their wives who were trying to reconnect and strengthen their marriages before the residents' release from prison. Other chaplains throughout the United States placed copies in their prisons' libraries.

Over the years, **GOD'S LADY** has gone into countries I have never visited. It has been read by troubled teens, ministry leaders of various denominations, and law enforcement professionals. Mothers have given it to their daughters. Men have read it and given it to the important ladies in their lives. To God be the glory for the great things He has done with that tiny book!

In music, a remix is a different version of an original recording. Since 1995, I have continued to study and teach about the value of godly womanhood, so I decided to make this book a remix of the original. It combines the original book's principles, primarily based on Proverbs 31, with vital expansions and additions. This book is a new and better version—a remix. With the increase in identity perplexities and misinformation among girls and women, I believe this message is more vital now than ever. God wants women to see themselves through His eyes. He wants them to embrace and enjoy every facet of their womanhood. God wants ladies to discover their gifts and enhance every skill entrusted to them. God also wants His ladies to display His love to every other female they encounter in ways that facilitate unity and synergy while eliminating envy and competition.

Please understand that this book is written "to" women, but not exclusively "for" women. Today, there are many men who are raising daughters alone. There are married men who want to uplift their wives and daughters. There are men who want to protect and pour into their female friends and relatives. There are honorable single men who want godly wives but don't know how to spot one. Although I participate in and thoroughly enjoy women's events, I believe until we make men aware of the information shared at these events, the wisdom and knowledge imparted will produce limited fruit. Men can't be helpful to females if the tools they need are withheld from them. My prayer is that this book will provide the understanding they desire, as well as the direction they need.

So, I now present **GOD'S LADY, Becoming a Woman of God's Design through Soul-Care.**

The Quest

Throughout my lifetime, I have seen women struggle to "find" themselves. These women are in various seasons of their lives. Their races, cultures, ethnicities, spiritual development, educational achievements, political persuasions, and marital statuses are diverse. Nonetheless, they share one common concern: a lack of personal fulfillment and contentment.

This pursuit can be a typical part of the maturation process. It is only when this search is unfruitful that self-hatred, depression, and even suicidal ideations surface. This unmet need for intrinsic joy sometimes causes women to abandon their families and friendships. They may bounce from relationship to relationship, city to city, job to job, and even church (or religious experience) to church. Some attempt to numb the pain of this problem with drugs and alcohol. Others try to make themselves feel good about themselves by spending money they don't have to buy things they don't need to impress people who don't care.

I have met girls and women who found themselves with the wrong people and in the wrong places. Some subsequently ended up in prison. Yet, many didn't realize they were incarcerated in their souls and spirits long before they lost their physical freedom. Others have spent years in relationships that have gradually removed every bit of productivity and hope from their lives. The worst-case scenarios have been the precious lives lost to suicide and homicide.

All the abuse, debasement, and destruction were the results of their attempts to solve internal needs through external means. They tried to determine their value with tools that had little or no value. These women tried to make themselves beautiful from the outside in instead of from the inside out. So, rather than achieving a sense of wholeness, they continued to feel as though their lives were disarrayed like the pieces of a confusing puzzle.

Some of you reading this book have grown weary of trying to attain and maintain authentic peace and a sense of genuine satisfaction. Some of you have given up on the notion that you can have a life filled with delight. You may think I'm referring to some sort of "pie in the sky" fantasy life. Let me assure you, I am not.

Ladies, you cannot continue to live as you always have, yet expect positive change. You cannot continue wasting valuable, irretrievable time merely existing when you can thrive. Jesus came to give us abundant life. This is for NOW! Jesus never promised anything that He could not deliver, but He needs your cooperation and effort. Ladies, you must realize that bonafide "self-care" starts with "soul-care," and soul-care leads to tranquility, productivity, and optimum well-being.

Do I have all of the answers to your problems? No, but Jesus does. As you continue to read this book, open your heart to Him. He will speak if you're willing to listen. He will guide you if you're willing to follow His instructions.

What did I learn from this chapter?

_____

_____

_____

_____

_____

_____

_____

_____

_____

_____

_____

_____

Look a Little Closer

What do you see when you look in the mirror? Do you see the person who is really there, or do you only visualize what you would prefer to be reflected back at you?

Is your hair the right color, length, or texture? Is your skin the desired hue? Should your eyes be a different color, shape, or size? Why doesn't your nose look like your daddy's folks? Did you inherit your grandma's hips? Are your feet too large, flat, or small? Why aren't you taller, shorter, or thinner?

I have rarely met people (including myself) who have been totally satisfied with their physical appearance. Trends come and go as people frantically attempt to make themselves more attractive. At least, that is what their objective is supposed to be.

This continually occurs because society and the cultures therein have convinced us that the so-called "beautiful people" are also the "happiest people." Every visual medium (television, social media, magazines, etc.) spends billions of dollars annually to constantly feed our minds with their ideas of how we should look and the images we should portray. Because of this, many seek medical professionals to tuck in, suck out, remove, and implant anything and everything, from head to toe, to try to attain physical perfection. Some will even risk injury or death to attempt to look like someone other than themselves. Some have physically manipulated their bodies to the extent that their own parents would not recognize photos of them (especially by the time they filter out more imperfections). Years ago, this was mainly done by those over 50, but now, even teenagers are going under the knife and subjecting themselves to other invasive cosmetic procedures.

Those who choose not to go that route opt for the less expensive and dramatic manual modes of metamorphosis. Billions of dollars are spent annually on hair care, cosmetics, skincare, and other fads to help the purchaser create the illusion of what the world calls "beauty." Some are so insecure about themselves that they won't allow anyone (not even family and friends) to see them in their natural state. I am convinced that when people go to such extremes to hide or change their outside, they are really attempting to mask a far greater lack lurking beneath the surface.

Please don't misunderstand. I believe that we should always look our best. We should take care of our health and be aware of our physical appearance. Since none of us are flawless, there's nothing wrong with accentuating or enhancing ourselves. After all, our bodies are the temples of the Holy Ghost (1 Corinthians 6.19), and we represent our Lord. However, God has commanded us to be temperate and not extreme in our behavior (Galatians 5.23; 2 Peter 1.6). When we lose our temperance, we lose God's perspective. When we take measures to drastically alter rather than gently modify our appearance, we leave the boundaries of temperance. In this sense, boundaries are not designed to restrict but to be guidelines.

When we consciously or subconsciously convince ourselves that what we take off, put on, or physically change determines who we are and our worth, we deceive ourselves. We must realize that if physical beauty guaranteed happiness, those who possess it would also acquire a sense of contentment. Instead, these persons continually strive, at a nonstop pace, to maintain and readjust themselves to achieve the impossible: the perfect look. I refer to it as impossible because no matter how good it looks today, as trends change, it won't be good enough tomorrow. Also, as age and gravity continue to make their presence known, what was fixed today will have to be refixed repeatedly. The cycle is endless.

If you don't believe me, just research the lists of celebrity deaths over the past several years. Most easily met the world's standard of physical attractiveness. Many were young and still successful in their careers. Yet too many committed suicide or overdosed on drugs.

Sisters, let's be honest with ourselves. There are real facts we can't afford to forget. First of all, God never gave anyone the option of choosing their biological parents. He alone made that choice. Our parents may have willingly been intimate, but only God controlled our conception and, ultimately, our birth. God decided which traits would be recessive and which would be dominant. In His infinite wisdom, He determined every feature. God's formation of us was strategic and intricate. Each of us is uniquely and wonderfully created. God planned us even if our parents didn't (Psalm 139.14; Jeremiah 1.5).

Look a little closer and see the beauty within. God's lady focuses on the inward adorning of spiritual and moral strength, honor, and self-respect. Her attention is given to those characteristics that age cannot diminish, makeup can't highlight, and the latest fashions cannot accentuate. When she enters a room, she is not noticed primarily because of her hairstyle or apparel. God's lady stands out because of the glow of peace and pure inner beauty, which only the indwelling power of the Holy Spirit can impart.

What did I learn from this chapter?

_____

_____

_____

_____

_____

_____

_____

_____

_____

_____

_____

_____

_____

A Mother's Influence

Proverbs 31 is a narrative of information given to King Lemuel by his mother. No definitive information has been found regarding this king or his mother. Some Bible scholars postulate that he may have actually been King Solomon because of the similarities in the meanings of their names. Others speculate that he may have been from some neighboring country and that his mother was a daughter of Israel. Nonetheless, King Lemuel's mother obviously took to heart her God-given responsibility to train and instruct her son (Proverbs 22.6).

The King James Version of the Bible calls Proverbs 31 a prophecy. The American Standard Version calls it an oracle. Both terms imply that the King's mother imparted information that was divinely inspired and, therefore, of utmost value. Because of the expressed wisdom she used in sharing this instruction with her son, I believe she was a woman of prayer and consecration.

It is noteworthy to emphasize that the King's "mother" provided him with pertinent instruction regarding two of the most significant areas of his life: his personal and professional life. Where was his father? Since his actual identity isn't clear, it cannot be determined if his father was dead, alive, ill, or just unavailable to instruct his son, the King. Yet, what can be ascertained is that God chose to use his mother to impart these life-impacting instructions.

Ladies, this confirms the fact that God speaks to and through us. God is not sexist. From a spiritual perspective, He does not primarily see people as male or female (Galatians 3.28). By no means does this diminish the roles and responsibilities of fathers. However, God reserves the right to use any submitted vessel that will obey and bring Him glory, regardless of gender. This oracle was meaningful not only for King Lemuel but also for every man and woman wise enough to read and utilize its contents.

Another valid point is that the King obviously had unquestionable respect for his mother. A man of his social and political status would need to have solid reverence and confidence in anyone who attempted to give him advice to avoid jeopardizing either position.

Mothers, we have God-given influence over our children, from the womb to the grave. Because of this, we must ensure that the advice we give is Christ-centered and biblically sound. We must never use our influence to meddle or manipulate.

In the first couple of verses of Proverbs 31, King Lemuel's mother appeared to ponder the best way to communicate the information God gave her for her son. I do not believe that her repetitive "what" referred to the content of her message because it came from God. But there are times when we, mere humans, struggle to find the appropriate words that will allow us to communicate a supernatural message with the same clarity and inspiration with which it was given and received. A credible message communicated with hasty or unseasoned words can obscure or even kill the content. Timing is also crucial. When God gives us instructions for another, we must be sure to share it at "the appointed time." Saying the right thing at the wrong time can also be damaging. We are required to seek God in prayer for guidance so that we say the right thing in the best way and at the correct time.

The phrases "my son," "son of my womb," and "son of my vows" are expressions of endearment. King Lemuel's mother was about to instruct him regarding two significant areas of his life. These expressions depict her maternal instinct to nurture him even though he was King. As mothers, that quality is often most apparent when we advise or assist our children in situations that are worthy of special attention.

The sequence of the mother's instructions is notable (Proverbs 31.3-9.) First, she advised him regarding his personal life. She told him how he should conduct himself publicly and privately. Then she told her son how he should perform specific areas of his kingly responsibilities. All this instruction was given *before* he was told what to look for in a wife. This indicates that a man who does not have his own matters in order is not qualified to be a husband. This order was established in the beginning. Adam had a place to live, a job, and a relationship with God before God gave him Eve (Genesis 2.7-25).

The woman described in Proverbs 31 is uncommon. She's not ordinary. She does not blend in but stands out. Women who demonstrate high morals, self-respect, and spiritual strength are attracted to men with similar attributes. A man exhibits his ability to lead a wife by the way he leads his own life. So again, the order of the instructions was deliberate and planned.

Throughout my life, I have met women who had the potential to accomplish great things in the Kingdom of God and society. To their detriment, they connected themselves to visionless men, who not only did nothing with their lives but discouraged these women from expanding their God-given abilities. These women were reduced to mere shells of who they could have become. Some were victims of all kinds of abuse by their husbands. They never had a husband to encourage and guide them towards the greatness they were capable of. Some died young due to health challenges that were possibly caused or at least intensified by their lives of turmoil. All lived unfulfilled and with many regrets.

Single ladies, you cannot afford to connect yourself with men who diminish rather than add to who you are. You may be able to teach him how to match his clothes, but you can't teach him how to be honest, dependable, secure, and holy. No one knows the heart of a person but God. The Lord knows who he is today and who he will be in ten, twenty, or fifty years. "Til death do us part " can seem like a torturous eternity when you are in covenant with someone you chose rather than the one God has prepared and approved. Also, God's not trying to "figure out" who's right for you. He already knows because His plans for you (and him) were established before you were conceived. Pray, then obey. If God says "no," walk away. When the Lord is silent it either means "wait" or "you already know that man is not a suitable mate." It would be better for you to cry for 30 days, rather than for 30 years. If He says "yes" then move forward.

Married women, if your husband is not Spirit-led and God-focused, you must tirelessly intercede for him. Pray that Jesus will draw him to salvation and transform his heart. Pray for your marriage daily. You can't nag him to the cross. Your constant criticizing and complaining won't give him a hunger for Jesus. Be wise. Love him. Honor him. Be the kind of mate you want him to be for you.

As mothers, we tend to instruct our children in areas of their lives that concern us. Our guidance focuses on those situations we don't believe they have gained the insight, wisdom, or maturity necessary to handle them effectively and efficiently.

Scripture doesn't indicate how long the son had been King or the quality of his reign. He may have been an inexperienced novice, still trying to settle into his role, or one with some experience, who needed to improve his leadership skills and get his personal life in order. Nevertheless, since God never gives direction haphazardly, the counsel provided was designed to empower him to be a man of godly principles and an exemplary leader.

Mothers, taking our rightful positions in God's Kingdom begins with our families. We are obligated to share our insight and information with our natural and spiritual offspring. We have a duty to allow those whom God has placed in our sphere of influence to benefit from all the lessons we have learned from our life experiences. Think about all the pitfalls, bad decisions, and headaches you could have avoided if someone had taken time to instruct you. Also, think of all the drama and stress you could have dodged if you had listened to the instruction given. We cannot force our adult children to heed our advice, but if we refuse to offer it, we leave them open to the anti-Christian advice of the world and make them vulnerable targets for the enemy of their souls.

We must never model the parenting procedures of the ungodly. The family is God's institution. The Bible is His instruction manual. God has given us a marvelous role model: King Lemuel's mother.

What did I learn from this chapter?

God's Lady Deserves a King

Several years ago, a mother told me she was praying that Jesus would give her single sons virtuous wives. My response was not what she expected or wanted. I told her God wouldn't do that until they qualified for such a wife…and He didn't.

For almost every promise stated in the Bible, there are prerequisites. Even for salvation, there is the prerequisite of faith. So God won't release an extraordinary woman to a substandard man, for it takes an exceptional man to lead and cover an authentic woman of virtue.

Just as the head serves as the "control tower" in the human body, the man is the control tower of the husband/wife relationship. He is the head: the leader of the marriage, just as Christ is to His bride, the Church (Ephesians 5.23-29). Therefore, the husband is to be the leader in prayer, spiritual warfare, worship, love, good stewardship, and integrity. The husband is to be a reflection of Christ.

Please note that the husband is the head of "his wife," not all women. The wife is instructed to support and revere "her husband." Also, although Jesus is the head of the Church, He is not a dictator. He draws us to Him with His pure and unconditional love, yet He allows each person to choose to be part of His bride. He does not force Himself on anyone, even though He sacrificed His life for everyone. The Lord has provided us with a clear blueprint for marriage.

In the human body, if the head suffers injury, disease, or deformity, the rest of the body is negatively impacted. No matter how strong and healthy the rest of the body may appear, it cannot operate at its peak with an injured head.

Correspondingly, marriages suffer when the "head" is not functioning at his best. The deficits may be self-inflicted or the result of outside intrusions. They may have evolved or happened abruptly. Nevertheless, when the head of the marriage is not healthy, the marriage needs rehabilitative care. This can be facilitated through prayer, fasting, study of the Word, sound counsel, and communication between the spouses through the guidance of the Holy Spirit.

As previously stated, King Lemuel's mother explained what was expected of him before she told him what to expect from a wife. Let's examine this information in Proverbs 31.3-9. First, the King's mother told him not to give his strength to women. In other words, she was telling him not to waste his time and energy "chasing skirts." While she may have been specifically referring to foreign/heathen women, the principle applies to random sexual encounters of every type. The more time men (and women) spend pursuing such idle encounters, the more their flesh drives them away from God's plans. This results in being guided by the lust of the eye and the lust of the flesh rather than the Word and Spirit of God (Galatians 5.16-17; 1 John 2.16). When lust controls a man's choices, genuine love cannot develop. Relationships built on lust don't last. Once the novelty subsides, a new pursuit ensues.

King Lemuel's mother instructed her son not to give himself to ways that destroy kings. He was to avoid anyone and anything that had the potential to diminish, obscure, or destroy his reputation as a leader. Leaders tend to be scrutinized more due to their positions. Those they lead need to have confidence in them so they can submit to their authority. When the trust of a leader is broken with the people, it is extremely difficult, if not impossible, to regain.

King Lemuel was advised against consuming strong drink: alcoholic beverages. As we know, alcohol dulls the senses, loosens the tongue, and decreases inhibitions. His mother stated that the consumption of strong drink could cause him to forget the principles he was obligated to uphold and negatively affect his ability to be a just and fair ruler. I believe her underlying message was that her son was too valuable and his position too impactful for him to risk losing all he had achieved because of something as nonessential as alcohol. She further explained that alcohol was suitable for those who were down and out, those who had little to look forward to in life.

We know the negative impact alcohol consumption can have on one's life. Even without being legally intoxicated, people often say and do things differently when under the influence. Besides, Spirit-filled Believers have God's indwelling power to energize, teach, comfort, and guide them— all without adverse side effects or hangovers. The bottom line is whether or not drinking alcohol enhances or diminishes one's relationship with Jesus and one's ability to be a suitable Kingdom representative.

King Lemuel's mother encouraged her son to be sympathetic, valiant, honest, righteous, and assertive. These qualities are inclined to attract and keep the attention of any honorable woman.

A sympathetic man is concerned about the welfare of others. He is not harsh or insensitive but kind-hearted. He seeks to comfort those less fortunate in their times of need.

A valiant man takes a firm stand for the principles he believes in. He protects his family and community. He demonstrates courage even when opposed. He is an example of true manliness, not brute force.

An honest man is concerned about obtaining and maintaining

the respect of others, especially those he loves and leads. His wife doesn't have to worry about whom or what he spends his time and money on. His words are his bond in his home and community. His family does not have to drop their heads in shame because of his behavior but can hold them high with admiration and regard.

A righteous man hungers and thirsts after those things that facilitate a strong and consistent relationship with God and his family. His primary pursuit is to seek the Kingdom of God and His righteousness. Because of this, God provides everything else he and his family need (Matthew 5.6, 6.33).

An assertive man is energetic. He is not lazy. He is a self-starter. He is proactive rather than reactive. He does what is expected rather than what's inspected. His wife does not have to carry unnecessary burdens because he provides for his family to the best of his ability.

After reading the Scriptures referenced, you may feel they don't apply to your husband. Your husband may not hold a high position. He may not be a political official. He may not be known by the masses. However, if he is a blood-cleansed, Spirit-filled man, he holds the highest and most prestigious status a man can obtain, for he is a "man of God." That title is not just reserved for clergy. He is part of a royal priesthood and chosen generation (1 Peter 2.9). He has God-given authority and Kingdom responsibilities to fulfill.

Ladies, when we understand what God expects from our husbands, we will not make unrealistic demands of them. We can then be supportive and inspiring, which will empower us to be effective helpmates rather than hurt-mates. God's systematic design for husband/wife relationships results in a harmonious flow of mutual appreciation, reverence, and adoration.

I cannot end this chapter without addressing a common problem in our society. Some single women refer to their sons as "the man of the house." Not only is this erroneous, but it can also be injurious to the mother-son relationship. The man of the house takes care of the needs of the home. He is the primary financial provider. He keeps the home and its inhabitants safe. He is responsible for the overall welfare of the family. Unless your son is an adult who does all these things, he is **not** the man of the house but your "son" for whom you are responsible. It is unwise to give him such a title when he is incapable of fulfilling the mandated duties. As it is, too many sons have limited knowledge of "godly manhood." This does not help.

The number-one consequence I have seen, as a result of telling sons this, manifests when a man becomes interested in the mother. I have seen sons sabotage these relationships because they viewed the new man as a competitor for the attention and love of the mother. In cases when the mother got married, the son saw himself as equal to the new husband in terms of status and authority. Extreme disrespect and resentment of the new husband's God-given authority as the leader of the family also occurred. Even if the son is an adult, he is still the mother's son, not her "man." It is extremely difficult to bring harmony to these relationships when the foundation has been faulty due to years of parental misguidance. The key to harmonious relationships in these cases depends upon how the mother initially defines the roles and responsibilities of her children when there is no man involved and then the dynamics established between both adults and the children as a family.

What did I learn from this chapter?

_____

_____

_____

_____

_____

_____

_____

_____

_____

_____

_____

_____

_____

The Two Josephs

There are many examples of men, chronicled in the Bible, who exemplify kingly qualities, but we will discuss only two. Even though neither were kings, they were leaders in their own right. Some of their noteworthy qualities go beyond those specifically mentioned in Proverbs 31. They are Joseph, the son of Israel (Jacob), and Joseph, the male guardian of Jesus Christ and husband of Mary.

Joseph, the son of Israel, was unique from his youth (Genesis 37, 39-50). One of his kingly qualities was his servant's heart. Joseph had a lifetime of admirable service to others. As a teenager, he served his father. As a slave in Potiphar's house, he served his master with nobility. Because of Joseph's integrity and skill, Joseph was not merely a slave but managed the entire household. Until Potiphar's wife lied, Potiphar trusted Joseph without reservation.

That lie resulted in Joseph's incarceration. While in prison, even though he was there unjustly, Joseph maintained his uprightness. Joseph's character earned him the confidence and favor of the head jailer, resulting in another promotion. Joseph wasn't just a prisoner but managed all of the other prisoners.

Joseph ultimately ended up in the palace of Pharoah. God gave Pharoah a problem and allowed Joseph to be the only one who could solve it. Subsequently, Joseph was elevated to his ultimate place of destiny: second in command in Egypt. At this juncture, Joseph's character was tested maximally when his family came to buy grain from him during the famine. Although his brothers initially conspired to kill him, he sustained their lives. Though his brothers originally hated him, he continued to love them. Instead of bitterness, Joseph demonstrated forgiveness. Rather than revenge, he showed mercy.

Throughout Joseph's life, recurring themes spoke of his kingly qualities. The first one was that the Lord was with Joseph. God was with Joseph in his father's house. God was with Joseph in the pit, then in Potiphar's house. God was with Joseph in prison, and God was with Joseph in the palace. Because God was with him, he had influence and success wherever he went. From the worst situation to the greatest, Joseph was entrusted with the possessions and lives of others.

The second recurring theme was that Joseph respected authority and, therefore, was given authority. In each stage of his life, Joseph was second in command. However, he was always effective and honorable. Each task he was assigned was performed with excellence. God (and his superiors) would not have entrusted him with greater ones if he had not performed the small tasks well. I often say, "If you're too big for small assignments, you're too small for big assignments." As a result, Joseph's kingly qualities allowed him to transition from a boy to a man and from a man to a ruler.

There is limited information in Scripture about this next Joseph, whose life we will examine (Matthew 1.18-25, 2.12-23; Luke 2.1-7). He did not appear to have a position of leadership in his community. He did not come from a wealthy or famous family. Nonetheless, Joseph was hand-picked by God for one of the most significant and noteworthy assignments in history: to be the male guardian of Jesus Christ and the husband of the woman who would give birth to the Messiah. (He must be referred to in this manner because we know that God was Jesus' Father.) No other man has ever, or will ever, have this unique responsibility placed upon his shoulders.

The kingly qualities of this Joseph were demonstrated through his leadership of his family. When he became aware that Mary (to whom he was engaged at that time) was pregnant, he handled the situation with discretion and compassion. During that era, under the laws and customs of the Jews, engagements were legally binding. If Joseph had exposed her pregnancy to the community, she would have been publicly humiliated and possibly stoned to death (Leviticus 20.10). Instead, he decided to quietly end the engagement. However, after the angel informed him of the supernatural conception Mary experienced, along with the identity of the Holy Child in her womb, Joseph did not doubt or question the message. He married Mary as planned and embraced his new responsibilities.

Joseph was a law-abiding man. He and a very pregnant Mary traveled from Nazareth to Bethlehem because the Emperor called for a census, which required everyone to go to their city of nativity. Little did the Emperor know that his census would cause prophecy to be fulfilled. Joseph obeyed the law and did not dodge the census because Mary was about to give birth. He did not leave her behind because of her physical condition. He kept her by his side. Joseph provided for and protected Mary and the precious Gift inside her womb.

Joseph demonstrated unwavering faith and obedience. Through a series of dreams, he was instructed to move his new family from Bethlehem to Egypt, then to Israel, and finally to Nazareth. Although the primary goal was to preserve Jesus' life, each move fulfilled prophecy (Matthew 2). Joseph was a man of immediate action. Nowhere in the Bible was there any implication of procrastination. Joseph took no detours or shortcuts. He did not add to or take away from the directives but listened and followed through quickly and precisely, even naming the baby Jesus as instructed. An important lesson we learn from Joseph is to just do what God says...period.

Joseph's life was not one of glamor or convenience. Every aspect of Joseph's assignment was awkward and disruptive. Marrying a woman who was already pregnant presented Joseph with new and unfamiliar challenges. Though he knew the origin of the baby, the masses did not. Even in Bible days, people were people. As Mary's belly grew, no doubt Joseph had to deal with rumors and whispers of gossip. He could not defend himself or Mary, nor was he instructed to tell anyone their "secret."

Most of us would have blown it right there. We would have felt compelled and justified to defend ourselves and clear things up. However, there are times when ridicule is part of the assignment. There are instances when we cannot defend our character. Those are the times when we must hold our peace and let the Lord vindicate us.

Traveling on the back of a donkey with a pregnant woman was an inconvenience in itself. It had to be uncomfortable for Mary. Considering that she was in the final days of her pregnancy, there were, without doubt, frequent stops (for a host of pregnancy-related reasons), which probably prolonged the trip. Not being able to find an appropriate place for them to stay and for Mary to give birth was another problematic situation. No one would ever choose to give birth in a smelly barn with animals and then place their newborn in a trough where animals ate. Not to mention, the baby was not just a baby but the King of Kings. There was nothing royal or prestigious about this scene.

In addition, the extensive traveling during Jesus' early life was laborious and prohibited them from settling down. But to keep the Saviour safe, Joseph did it despite the inconvenience.

Joseph was a man who "forfeited his rights" to do what was right. When he initially thought Mary had been unfaithful to him, he had the legal right to make a spectacle of her and have her executed. Yet, Joseph did not seek vengeance but chose to extend grace.

When he married Mary, he forfeited his right to sexual intimacy with her, until after Jesus was born. I don't see in Scripture where he was instructed to do that. I believe Joseph made that decision so that the paternity of Jesus could never be questioned, although no one else was with them during that part of their journey.

Last, but not least, Joseph was sober-minded and humble. His ego never got in the way of his mission. Not being the "main attraction" didn't matter. He realized that his Kingdom calling was to ensure that Mary fulfilled hers. Joseph also understood that he and Mary were responsible for the care and upbringing of Jesus—the actual main attraction. Because of this, God could trust him as a suitable guardian of His only Begotten Son. Even now, Joseph doesn't get much attention in sermons or teachings, but he is a man from whom we can glean many valuable lessons.

Some of the kingly qualities demonstrated by the two Josephs include:
- Their relationships with God were firm.

- Both of them were level-headed and honorable.

- Their unique Kingdom assignments placed them in multiple life-and-death situations.

- They led and protected their families.

- They were kind-hearted.

- They were courageous despite the severity of the odds they faced.

- Because they followed God's instructions, lives were spared.

A man who loves God is worth loving. A man who follows God can lead others. A man who respects authority can be given authority. A man who does what's necessary rather than what's convenient is destined for success. A man who puts his destiny before his desires isn't just a man but a kingly man.

Ladies, a man who can press 300 pounds may be strong physically, but if he's fragile mentally, spiritually, and morally, he's not the king you need to lead you and your family. Don't settle for a man who can buy you a car but doesn't have compassion. Don't seek a man who can take you on vacation but can't take you into the presence of Jesus. Don't fall for a man who wants a family but won't protect and care for it. If you're married, you can't discard your husband, but now you know the traits you must pray for him to seek and cultivate.

What did I learn from this chapter?

_____

_____

_____

_____

_____

_____

_____

_____

_____

_____

_____

_____

_____

Women and Rubies

Proverbs 31:10 says, "Who can find a virtuous woman? For her price is far above rubies." The term "virtuous woman" was translated from the Hebrew word *chayil* (pronounced khah'-yil). It refers to a lady who demonstrates strength mentally, morally, and spiritually. I prefer the King James Version of this Scripture because it compares this exquisite woman to rubies.

The ruby has been called the most precious gemstone created by God. It is mentioned throughout the Bible. In India, it has been called the "king of precious stones." In Europe, the ruby has been used in coronation rings and in the crowns of Christian monarchs. Mining for rubies is perilous, but because of their value, miners take the risks. Wars have been fought, and thefts have occurred to obtain these precious gemstones.

Let's compare and contrast the qualities of the *chayil* woman and rubies.

- **No two rubies are alike.** God intentionally designed each woman to be unique. Because she is fearfully and wonderfully made, she must see herself (as well as other women) as designer's originals rather than bargain basement knockoffs or valueless hand-me-downs (Psalm 139.14).

- **Fine-quality rubies of greater than one carat are rare.** The price increases significantly as the size increases. Rubies can command the highest per-carat price of any colored gemstone. The virtuous woman is indeed rare in this world that devalues spiritual, mental, and moral strength. The qualities that make her valuable originate from within. Her value isn't determined by the size of her bank account but by the substance of her character. Her worth increases as she continually allows God to infiltrate every area of her spirit woman. Like a fine artistic masterpiece, God's lady becomes more priceless with age.

- **Rubies have inclusions, which are materials, such as crystal particles, trapped inside the stone during its formation.** The inclusions affect the structure and appearance of the gem. Whereas in other gemstones, inclusions may decrease their value, for these rare and exquisite gems, inclusions confirm their authenticity, add to their beauty, and increase their value. The *chayil* woman is not flawless. She has imperfections. Nonetheless, because she is submitted to Jesus and led by the Holy Spirit, she doesn't look like what she's been through. God allows those imperfections to add to, rather than lessen, her worth. Because she loves God and is called according to His purpose, He makes all things work together for her good (Romans 8.28).

- **The most outstanding characteristic of the ruby is its radiant red color.** The color red has historically been associated with wealth, passion, power, and success. In the Christian world, red is a reminder of the atoning blood of Jesus and the suffering He endured because of His unconditional love for mankind. So, the color red represents "redemption." Some often overlooked definitions of redemption or redeem are: to make worthwhile; to change for the better; to repair; to restore. God's lady makes everything she touches worthwhile. She makes a house, a home. She can take random items in the refrigerator and present her family with a gourmet meal. This woman can stretch two weeks' worth of income to cover a month's worth of debts. The *chayil* woman is often the glue that holds her family together, as well as the repairer of broken relationships. Through prayer and following God's principles, the virtuous woman brings harmony where there is chaos. She speaks life and brings restoration to dead situations. She may not have the best of everything by the world's standards, but she always gives her best to everything and everyone.

It is indeed a compliment to be compared by God to one of the most precious, distinctive, uncommon, and beautiful gemstones of His creation: the ruby. The world says that diamonds are a girl's best friend. But I have become especially partial to rubies because they remind me of how God sees His ladies.

What did I learn from this chapter?

_____

_____

_____

_____

_____

_____

_____

_____

_____

_____

_____

_____

The Chayil Woman

Proverbs 31:10-31 describes an incredible woman. This is the kind of woman King Lemuel's mother instructed him to pursue. She's not a supermodel or actress. She is not an athlete or politician. But she is a woman of dignity, grace, and godliness. Her physical characteristics are not mentioned. Her beauty is defined and manifested through the qualities of her soul and spirit. There is nothing that this woman is—that every woman who commits her life to Christ—cannot be. Sisters, despite all our racial, financial, educational, and physical differences, we all have the ability to be "more than just women." We can be God's ladies, *chayil* women: women fit for kings.

The *chayil* woman is more valuable than costly gems (see Women and Rubies). In our society, men and women will borrow, scrape, and steal for things of great value.

Consider the masterpieces that originated from the great artists of the past. People of every generation appreciate their uniqueness and distinctiveness. Novices tirelessly study them in an attempt to capture the techniques that make them captivating. Their attraction and monetary value continue to spiral upward with each year of their existence. Keep in mind this typically holds true only for originals, not duplicates.

God sees the *chayil* woman from this perspective. God made every one of His ladies from an original mold. His intricate creation of each of them was masterfully planned. Whereas they may have commonalities, they are each one of a kind. Her individuality makes her stand out in any crowd. She is cherished and highly esteemed by her Creator.

Ladies, why do so many of us devalue ourselves when God regards us so highly? Some women only see themselves as outlets for the uncensored animalistic appetites of men. Others view themselves as slaves and breeders. Too many women have no clear picture of their identity or worthiness. Not understanding an item's value often causes it to be misused or discarded. Yet when the quality of a distinctive and precious item is recognized, it's handled with care. These principles also hold true relative to how we should treat ourselves (and others) and how we allow ourselves to be treated. It's time for all of us to take a good, hard look at ourselves through the eyes of God and adjust our perspectives accordingly.

Without doubt, I believe there are women who will read this book who are or have been victims of every kind of abuse known to mankind: physical, sexual, mental, psychological, and spiritual. Yes, I said spiritual abuse. I define spiritual abuse as the kind of gross mistreatment that is initiated and perpetuated by spiritual leaders (male and female). These leaders cause their victims to feel spiritually powerless. They promote themselves as spiritually superior, thus convincing their victims to rely on them rather than Jesus. They are manipulative, dominating, and cruel. They typically find their targets among the broken and vulnerable. Distorted teaching and the misuse of Scripture are their greatest tools of deception. There is nothing in the Word of God that supports this maltreatment. This is why it is paramount that each individual cultivate and maintain their own viable relationship with our Lord. We are to follow our leaders as they follow Christ (1 Corinthians 11.1).

Your abuser may provide you with your basic necessities and even a few luxuries, but are these things worth your peace of mind? You may appear to be living the "American dream," but are you living according to God's principles and plans? Ladies, your dignity and well-being should never be exchanged for wealth or status. You were not created to be a punching bag, garbage dump, or hired hand.

I am not advocating the dissolution of families. Nevertheless, I am advocating Bible-based, Christ-centered, Holy Spirit-driven relationships. Your husband is commanded to love you just as Christ loves the Church (Ephesians 5. 25, 28). Jesus doesn't love the Church because she is flawless, but despite her flaws. Then, He empowers each Believer to continually mature and become more like Him. Any man who does not have a sound relationship with God will struggle with his relationship with you, even if he isn't abusive. Only God can empower the husband to mirror the love of Jesus and see you as He does. Jesus doesn't exploit, mishandle, or oppress His Bride. Every husband is expected to follow His example.

It is apparent from Scripture that the *chayil* woman is busy and productive. Some women are constantly in motion, but their activities don't yield good fruit. God's lady is successful in every area of her life because her priorities are in harmony with the principles of God. Without doubt, her first priority is God. Only He can empower her to be an extraordinary wife, mother, businesswoman, and Kingdom servant. She has it all.

Ladies, I have been abundantly blessed to "have it all," too. I have been a wife, mother, career woman, and minister. The reason why God prospered each of these areas was because of how I correctly prioritized my life. Before my husband and I married, we spent time fasting and praying to be sure that our union was God-ordained. I never took a professional position without seeking God's approval. Throughout my career, very lucrative and prestigious offers were placed in my lap. Whereas they were good, they were not from God. In some cases, those positions would have taken me out of town too often when my children were young. One position was discontinued a few years after I was approached. If I had taken it, I would not have had the opportunities promised.

I did not neglect my husband or children in the name of "ministry," for I realized they were my **first** ministry and responsibility. Please understand that nothing in my life suffered when I turned opportunities down. God would always send another unexpected blessing that would allow me to fulfill and enjoy all my responsibilities.

We have to know when to say "no!" We can't let pride, vanity, or money lure us into opportunities that are not assignments. We can have it all, but we must discern the times and seasons of our lives. Priorities must be adjusted in lieu of a given season. Children need your presence, time, and training when they are young. When you have a husband, you can't be married to your career or your ministry.

A word to all the single ladies…

Being single does not make you inferior to married women, and getting married won't make you superior to anyone. Being married to a godly man is wonderful. I was married to an amazing man for twenty years before he passed. I have been single for twenty-five years. With God's help, I finished raising two children, who are now productive adults, and I am the grandmother of a delightful grandson. I lived a full life before my marriage. I lived a gratifying life while married, and my life continues to be fruitful and exciting. My point is that your marital status should not determine the quality of your life. Singleness should not be an excuse to postpone achieving goals and experiencing everything God has planned for this season of your life. As a matter of fact, your single season is your best time of exploration, evolution, and service.

Now, I need to address those ladies over sixty…

That Medicare card doesn't diminish your value. You're still a *chayil* woman. You may be retired from working, but God has not given you permission to retire from living! Boredom is not a mandatory requirement of aging. You are still above the dirt, so make good use of every day. Don't doubt yourself or the God in you. God has kept you on earth because you still have contributions to make to society and the Kingdom.

Your children may be grown and living their lives independently of you. Well, now you can live your life independently of the parental responsibilities that tied you down when they were young. If you are married, you and your husband have the freedom to enjoy each other from a different vantage point. If you are single (divorced, widowed, or never married), you now have the freedom to be the best version of the "mature you." There may be some things you can't do anymore, but there are still many things you can experience and enjoy. Do what you can while you can. Continue to bloom! Have fun!

Seasoned ladies, please understand that your "mothering" days may not be over. Throughout my professional and ministry travels, I have frequently met girls and women who have been managed but not mothered. They have information but no wisdom. They have been catered to but not properly corrected. They have been entertained but not nurtured. Some of these women are middle-aged, chronologically but teenagers, mentally and emotionally. They need exposure to a side of womanhood absent from their life experiences. They need you! There are girls and women who need to know the positive and negative lessons you've learned. You need to tell them about your challenges and victories. They need a mature woman to tell and show them they don't have to become negative statistics. They need to recognize they can allow their setbacks to be barriers or stepping stones. Ask God to bring those into your life to whom you are assigned. If He does not bring anyone specifically to you, you can be an anonymous intercessor for these women. In doing so, your life will be a testimony to others long after you enter eternal rest. When it's time for you to leave earth, you should depart with nothing left to give—you should be **empty**.

The husband of the *chayil* woman can completely trust her with his heart. She gives him no reason to seek sexual or emotional fulfillment elsewhere. Let's look at this in detail. Contrary to what society says, God created sexual intimacy to be experienced and enjoyed within the context of a heterosexual marriage. Sex is not nasty. Sex, in its proper context, is not lust. Lust is one's strong sexual desire for someone other than their spouse. Lust is also the root of sexual desires that are not in alignment with the guidelines of God's Word, specifically sexual activities that humiliate or harm the spouse in some way. Husbands are supposed to desire their wives passionately. Wives should have sexual desire for their husbands. That's what God ordained and expects. It was not created for dating. Sex is not legitimate during the engagement period. God didn't create this unique expression of love to be experienced through the perversion of pornography. Since God is the creator of sex, only He has the right to determine how, when, and with whom it is experienced.

Hebrew 13.4 says, "*Marriage is honorable in all and the bed undefiled; but whoremongers and adulterers God will judge.*" That means marriage is to be respected and held in high regard by everyone. The marriage bed (sexual intimacy) is to be unpolluted, held sacred, and pure. Even the marriage vows echo this sentiment, for the couple promises mutual fidelity. Whoremongers and adulterers are those who engage in sexual activities that aren't in harmony with the Scriptures (1 Corinthians 7.2-3). Just as God is the creator of sex, He is also the ultimate judge of sin; therefore, He has the authority to condemn illicit sexual conduct.

The Bible describes satan as a thief who comes to steal, kill, and destroy (John 10.10). Sex is one of the primary areas in which he is constantly at work to fulfill his mission. The enemy has worked tirelessly to steal sex from marriage and interjected it into every other relationship on earth. All forms of sexual abuse continue to increase in our society. Respect for godly human sexuality is at an all-time low. Sexual images flood every medium of entertainment to the extent that even some Christians don't have (or don't enforce) spiritually healthy boundaries for what they ingest through the media. When it comes to sex, many people have become reprobate: no filters, no consciousness, and no restraint.

Because of this, the enemy has killed people. I am sure most readers can recall someone who has suffered or died from a sexually transmitted disease. Many years ago, an acquaintance, who was a medical professional, told me that blood tests were discontinued as a criterion for getting a marriage license because candidates were only tested for syphilis and gonorrhea. The types and potency of sexually transmitted diseases increased so rapidly that it became too expensive to try to test marriage license applicants for all of them. In addition, many of the typical medications were no longer beneficial in treating these conditions. That was in 1980! Since then, more diseases have manifested, and more people have been negatively impacted.

Satan's sexual agenda has not only destroyed individual lives but entire families and the moral fiber of the world. I have encountered children who were not old enough to drive a car but had more sexual partners than people twice their age. Some had been exposed to STDs that could prove to be fatal during their middle school years. Because of fear, immaturity, and ignorance, there were those who refused to seek medical treatment.

The laws of many states endorse these behaviors. A person can have HIV/AIDS and compel their doctors, in the name of privacy and confidentiality, to withhold that information from their spouse. I had an acquaintance who was married to a man who contracted AIDS and kept it from her. She had no clue until he was almost dead. Eighteen months later, she died due to contracting AIDS from him. Common-law marriages are preferred by many over Bible-based covenants. Children can engage in sexual reassignment treatments without parental permission. Children who are too young to vote can legally engage in sexual relationships with adults who are old enough to be their parents.

When I conduct pre-marriage coaching, sexual history is a topic that is always addressed. I encourage couples to be frank about this. I give them the foundation, then allow them to discuss details privately. These conversations must take place before the marriage because many have lived in environments that did not teach God's plan for sex. Some have been sexually assaulted or abused. Others have sexual fears. Some individuals have sexual addictions that have not been remedied. Singles cannot be naive and think that everything will take care of itself after marriage. That's fantasy. You and your fiancé must discuss more than how many children you want, where you want to live, or your relationships with Christ. Not having a "meeting of the minds" regarding sex will cause one or both of you to bring heavy baggage into the marriage that should have been unpacked before the covenant was made.

God's lady does not use sex to manipulate her husband. She does not withhold sex to punish him. The *chayil* woman does not use sex as leverage or as a negotiation tool because she realizes that would reduce their relationship to that of a prostitute and patron. She respects his body and takes pleasure in expressing her love for him.

The husband of God's lady is emotionally secure because she honors him. His wife understands that she is his helpmate, not hurtmate. She does not compete with her husband but collaborates with him to attend to the needs of the family. Their destinies, aspirations, and dreams don't clash but complement each other.

In this era, honor appears to be a forgotten principle. It does not rank highly on the codes of conduct of many people. The Bible tells us to honor each other. However, too many people only want to be on the receiving end. Honor is not passive but powerful. Honor is not a sign of weakness since one who honors is strong and secure enough to edify another.

Ladies, I know your husband isn't flawless, but neither are you. He may not even be a Believer. Nonetheless, you must respect and honor his position that *you* gave him when you said, "I do," even when you disagree with his actions. Acts of honor are acts of kindness. Honor can do what criticism can't. Honor can change what harassment won't. Honor can turn his heart towards Christ when preaching at him doesn't. Honor can decrease discord. Honor can create a loving atmosphere, even in the absence of sex, because there are times when sex isn't feasible, but honor is always possible. In addition to all of that, honor begets honor.

God's lady is skillful with her hands. I envision her as someone who can take something simple and transform it into something splendid. She can take a "piece of this" and a "swatch of that" and create a masterpiece that evokes amazement and maybe even envy. Women who have this talent add value to everything they touch. Many such women function in the "ministry of helps." If given an assignment, it will be completed with excellence, down to the last detail. Also, she is a woman who doesn't have to be bribed or begged since she willingly attends to any task that's within her power to perform.

Proverbs 31 reveals that the *chayil* woman is an industrious entrepreneur. Her knowledge and skills touch diverse aspects of business, including merchandising, importing and exporting, real estate, agriculture, and tailoring. She may or may not have a college degree, but her skills indicate she can hold her own in the marketplace. Her business savvy empowers her to meet her family's and servants' financial needs. Her career enables her to assist her husband, not assassinate her family. She also shows us that career women were present in ancient Bible times. Even in that era, the "woman's place" was not limited to household chores. Deborah (wife, judge, and prophet), Pricilla (wife, tentmaker, and minister), and Lydia (businesswoman who sold luxurious purple textiles) are other noteworthy women of the Bible who were successful beyond the home.

God's lady ministers to those in need in the community. Because she has been blessed, she readily blesses others. This is an example of outreach ministry. I often hear women say they don't know what God wants them to do. Well, ministry is often discovered as we serve where we see a need. As we follow the example and instructions of Jesus, we will find our niche. Jesus may not reveal your ministry through an angelic visitation, word of prophecy, or bolt of lightning, but by simply presenting an opportunity to point a soul to Him or meet an obvious need. Visiting the sick, witnessing to the lost, providing comfort, feeding the hungry, and clothing the naked are just a few general ministry assignments given to all Christians. If Jesus wants you to do more, He will definitely tell you. Remember: God uses people who are involved, not sitting on the sidelines waiting to be summoned.

When I first gave my life to Christ, I was an excited young and single college student. I participated in everything available, including church clean-up crew, choir, youth ministry, evangelism, and Christian Education. Some specific areas of ministry were revealed as I engaged in these general ones. My career as a Speech-Language Pathologist was also an area of ministry because it allowed me to serve significant needs, which improved the quality of life of my students/patients. I learned how to write as a result of writing many comprehensive diagnostic reports. I became sensitive to the struggles and pain of others through my secular career. Because of my vocation, I learned patience when dealing with hurting people. Needless to say, it was a Holy Ghost set up for other specific areas of ministry in which I have humbly served over the past 50 years. To God be the glory!

According to this proverb, the *chayil* woman is a planner. She is proactive rather than reactive. She doesn't wait until it begins to snow but has everything prepared for her family before winter arrives. I believe the "winter season" represents more than just the time of year when frigid temperatures, snow, and ice are typical. As a mother, I perceive winter as any period of life that can cause extreme challenges or hardships: times of crisis. Obviously, one cannot plan for every winter-like season. Yet, God's lady takes forethought to attempt to insulate her family from the potential physical, emotional, economic, and spiritual hardships that can happen to anyone. That can only be done through prayer, hiding God's Word in her heart, and keeping her spiritual eyes and ears open.

A wise mother is her children's first teacher. Therefore, a significant part of her winter-season preparation is done through preparing her children for life. We know that children are more inclined to imitate our actions rather than merely follow our words. As her children observe her relationship with their father, homemaking, benevolence, and integrity, they also see the resulting favor of God upon her life.

Proverbs 31:22 implies she is aware of her appearance but not obsessed with it. Her clothing of silk and purple imply a look of sophistication and nobility. Remember, these qualities must first be cultivated in the heart. We must wear the correct undergarments to make an outfit look its best. At a formal event a few years ago, I saw a woman wear a costly evening gown with the wrong undergarments. What was under the dress made the dress look cheap and unflattering. I saw another woman wearing a less expensive dress. The dress fit perfectly and looked elegant because of what was under it. I'm sure you get the point.

Ladies, we represent some very significant people: Jesus, our husbands, our families, and ourselves. Each of them deserves the best representation we can give them. My children's friends know me primarily as Jayson's and Candace's mother. There are still people who mainly know me as Clarence's wife/widow. Whether I am distributing food, praying for the sick, or teaching doesn't matter. Those to whom I minister associate me mainly with Jesus Christ. Because I understand that my visual/physical impression is the first thing (and sometimes the only thing) others see, and it can impact everyone I love, I want it to be positive. Each of us has this responsibility. We may not wear the latest or most expensive fashions, but we can always be poised, polished, and powerful. God's lady doesn't attend to her appearance because she "wants" somebody but because she "is" somebody."

Not only does the *chayil* woman give her husband honor, but she causes him to be honored by others in their community (see v. 23). Just as a whorish wife causes shame, the virtuous wife brings prestige.

The woman King Lemuel's mother described is powerful yet gentle; bold but not overbearing; responsible but does not micromanage; and intelligent but not proud. When she speaks, others listen. They don't listen because of her extensive vocabulary or her loud volume. They listen because her words overflow with godly wisdom. Even when her words are corrective, they exemplify her genuine concern and desire to help others function at their peak.

When my children went through their rebellious years, there were times when I had to stand toe-to-toe with them. At one point, I doubted my effectiveness as a Christian parent. It seemed as though every godly seed my husband and I tried to instill in them had been plucked up. I looked to see signs of the Holy Spirit, who I knew indwelled them but seemed to be completely dormant. I remember the stressful nights of endless tears. I learned that "tough love" is often tougher on the parent than the child. I kept loving them, although there were times when I questioned their love for me. I continued to stand my ground, although, on occasion, it felt like quicksand. I ignored the chatter from others and ran my household in the manner I knew would please the Lord. It was not easy, and change did not happen overnight...but *change did happen.*

Because we endured and overcame our trials, our family is solid. God's Word has always been and will always be our foundation. Our family is joyful because the Lord's joy is indeed our strength. All of those years of testing birthed numerous testimonies. If you knew our struggles, you would understand our smiles. I can tell you from experience that if you pray and obey, victory will come.

Being a parent and wife are two of a woman's most demanding responsibilities. Love must be given for it to be reciprocated. Respect must be earned, not mandated. Don't let the world's system contaminate your family. God obligates Himself to His Word. If you follow His principles, He will back them (and you). Your family may not always understand you, but in the long run, they will "arise and call you blessed!"

Verse 30 of this Proverb spells out those things that are temporal as opposed to those that are lasting. The approval of people can change in the blink of an eye. One day, they love you, and the next day (sometimes the next hour) they hate you. Some will change their opinions for fickle reasons, while others will change just because that's their prerogative.

Outward beauty also has an expiration date. If all you have is your pretty face, shapely body, and expensive clothes, you don't have much. Yes, you can have plastic surgery. Yes, you can purchase the latest fashions. You can go to the gym daily. Yet you must remember that time and gravity will continue to reveal themselves from time to time. I have never seen a 60-year-old woman look as she did at 30. The key is not to try to recapture who you were but to be at your "now peak" regardless of your age.

A woman who is picture-perfect outwardly but dead spiritually does not possess the personal satisfaction and contentment that the Proverbs 31 woman enjoys. Too many women are on a non-ending quest to "beat the clocks" of age, changing fashions, and changing finances. Because the *chayil* woman reveres the Lord, He continues to beautify her each year from the inside out. Her glow of holiness and aura of peace cannot be diminished by the passing of time.

In the final verse, we are told that the *chayil* woman deserves public acclaim because of the things she does. Although she brings honor to her husband, God wants her to receive her own accolades. This woman can receive **and** give honor. She can be esteemed without looking down her nose at others who may not have accomplished as much as she. It's safe to presume that as she receives praise, she gives it back to God, for she knows that everything she has accomplished has been because of Him and for His glory!

Chayil women are "finishers." They don't half-do things or leave loose ends. *Chayil* women don't step on, pull down, or cast away others to gain or maintain the spotlight. They don't try to push themselves to the top because they understand from whom authentic elevation comes. Even in death, the *chayil* woman's life and legacy are remembered fondly. We must realize that our daily lives are our true obituaries. Regardless of what the eulogist says, people will remember us for our deeds, not our things.

What did I learn from this chapter?

_____

_____

_____

_____

_____

_____

_____

_____

_____

_____

_____

_____

_____

God Always Has a Witness

A noteworthy biblical principle states that nothing is confirmed without two or three witnesses (Matthew 18.16; 2 Corinthians 13.1). Because the woman of Proverbs 31 is a nameless ideal, I wanted to cite three specifically chronicled in the Bible who lived up to the standards depicted. They are Deborah, Esther, and the Shunammite woman.

Deborah was the only female judge of Israel (Judges 4 and 5). She was a wife, judge, and prophet. When she took her political position, Israel had been in bondage under King Jabin for 20 years. In response to the cries of the children of Israel, God gave Deborah a military strategy that ensured Israel's victory over its enemy.

The way Deborah handled this situation was exemplary. Although she was the judge, she followed proper protocol and discussed the God-given plan with the military commander, Barak. She didn't get cocky or go over his head. She demonstrated respect for his position.

Because Deborah demonstrated regard for Barak, it was reciprocated. Barak was not offended because God chose to reveal the needed strategy to Deborah instead of him. He was not threatened by Deborah. On the contrary, Barak trusted Deborah to the extent that he would not go into battle without her (Judges 4.8). He wasn't weak, but wise. Barack didn't allow gender, position, pride, customs, or experience to stand in the way of the job that needed to be completed. He wanted to win, and they did!

Not only did Deborah and Barak war together, but they worshiped together. What a commendable combination. Judges 5 tells us they composed and sang a song of praise and celebration describing their God-orchestrated victory. Because of Deborah's relationship with God, keen spiritual ears, and obedience to His instructions, Israel experienced 40 years of rest and peace. That's twice as long as they had been in bondage.

Ladies, everything we touch should become better. Actually, if we follow what I call the "Deborah principle," everything we touch should be twice as good. If we aren't changing things for the better, we may be adding to their contamination and destruction.

Let's focus our attention now on Esther. Esther was an orphaned Jewess raised and groomed for greatness by her cousin/adopted father, Mordecai (Book of Esther). Out of all the maidens in the running to be the next Queen, she was chosen. A study of the book, which bears her name, revealed her beauty initially caught the eye of King Ahasuerus, but her character captured and kept his heart. The Bible states that Esther was the most favored and loved of all her husband's wives. It's important to note that Esther took the place of Queen Vashti, who was also beautiful, but her personality and disposition caused her to lose her place of prominence.

Ladies, don't be deceived. There is absolutely nothing wrong with physical beauty. Yet those attributes that lie beneath the surface facilitate the most valuable, impactful, and long-lasting outcomes.

When Haman (the King's Prime Minister) schemed to kill the Jews, Esther, at the advice of Mordecai, risked her security, position, and life to save her people. Even though she broke traditional protocols to approach the King, it wasn't for impractical or selfish reasons but for the greater good. Because of her favor with her husband, the King listened to her, and ultimately the Jews were saved. Also, Hamon was exposed and executed, and Mordecai was placed in a new elevated position by the King.

One of Esther's most memorable attributes was her undying respect for Mordecai. Although she was Queen, she knew Mordecai was instrumental in her having that position, and she did not disregard him after attaining it. If someone's advice and wisdom helped you become successful, you may want to retain them in your circle. Too often, people "burn the bridges" they crossed to reach higher ground, not realizing they may someday have to cross those bridges again. Never forget those who the Lord allowed to help you during your struggles. If their counsel was worthwhile then, don't smugly disregard it now.

The Bible referred to Esther as a beautiful young virgin. During that time, most Jewish girls married between the ages of 12-14. Her youth made Mordecai's guidance even more essential. Mordecai helped her realize God had not allowed her to become Queen just to be "eye candy" for the King, but she had a Kingdom assignment that required her to be loyal to her people and divine purpose.

Women of God, you must understand that your family, business, and career are more than they seem on the surface. They are part of your personal Kingdom assignments. You may not be a queen in the formal sense, but you have God-given influence. You may not stop the annihilation of a race of people, but you may be assigned to prevent the destruction of your neighborhood. God can use you to expose the "Hamans" in your city.

The third woman is a bit different, but at the same time, quite similar to the previous two. In Scripture, she is called the Shunammite woman, which merely tells us that she was from a place called Shunem (2 Kings 4.8-36). The King James Bible calls her a "great woman," but the Amplified Bible refers to her as "prominent and influential." In a nutshell, she was well-known and had a distinguished reputation. She was a *chayil* woman in her own right.

Three of her outstanding qualities were kindness, hospitality, and honor. Each time the prophet Elisha visited her region, she fed him. After doing this for a while, she asked her husband if they could prepare a formal place for the prophet to lodge in their home. She wasn't satisfied with just providing a meal; she wanted to accommodate Elisha's needs further. According to the Bible, she placed a lamp, table, and bed in Elisha's room. The lamp and table would provide a place for Elisha to study and pray. The bed was for rest. So, this was not a vacation spot but a place of respite. Remember that Elisha didn't request this; she did it voluntarily.

Also, note that she showed her husband honor by consulting with him and getting his approval. Ladies, you can get more cooperation from your husbands when you work with them rather than around or above them. Even if you think he doesn't care about a given situation, it makes him feel valued when you take time to collaborate with him. When you make him feel as though his opinion is irrelevant, you make him feel worthless as a man.

Nowhere in Scripture does it indicate that the Shunammite woman discussed what she and her husband did for Elisha with anyone else. She didn't sound any trumpets. She didn't tell her friends and neighbors that the great prophet Elisha was her house guest. It appeared that everything she did was done privately. No doubt, if the townspeople had known, they would have flocked to her house to hear him prophesy or receive a miracle, which would have been counterproductive to providing a place of rest and solitude for the man of God.

As I read the account of the Shunammite woman, I thought of Matthew 10.41 (AMP), which says, *"He who receives and welcomes a prophet because he is a prophet will receive a prophet's reward; and he who receives a righteous (honorable) man because he is a righteous man will receive a righteous man's reward."* She did not ask for anything in return. Just being able to make Elisha's visits to Shunem more pleasant was thanks enough for her. The Shunammite woman told Elisha she didn't want anything, but he was compelled to do something special for her.

The blessings she and her husband received defied nature. These blessings were things that seemed impossible. The Bible says that the Shunammite woman and her husband had no children and specifically stated that her husband was old, not that she was barren. Therefore, the miracle was twofold: the husband's ability to father a child was restored, and their miracle son was born.

Ladies, look at the magnitude of the blessings reaped from the seeds of hospitality and honor that were sown. I often hear people say we can only receive the same harvest as the seed we sow. Well, that's true in the natural or physical realm, but that's not always the case in the realm of the Spirit. She gave food and lodging yet received the regeneration of her husband's virility and a son. With God, absolutely nothing is impossible!

The story does not end there because two more of the Shunammite woman's virtuous qualities were faith and tenacity, demonstrated in her behavior and language. There came a day when the Shunammite's miracle died. But being the *chayil* woman that she was, she refused to accept the demise of her heart's desire. The short version of the rest of the story is that she left her dead son at home and traveled until she found Elisha. As she left home in pursuit of the prophet, she told her husband, "It shall be well." But when she responded to Elisha's inquiry about her son, her words became more definitive, and she said, "It *is* well." Because of her persistence, Elisha returned home with her, and another miracle was manifested: the resurrection of the boy from the dead.

As *chayil* women, we can't be distracted or negatively influenced by our environment. We must be willing to believe God's promises and maintain them, even if it means resurrecting them from dead places.

Let's examine some of the similarities of these three women.

- They were problem solvers, not problem causers.

- They were not swayed by the severe circumstances of their crises.

- They were women of order and protocol.

- They were women of integrity.

- They knew how to honor and work with men.

- They knew how to ask for help.

- They were respectful and respected.

- Specifically, Deborah and Esther knew how to handle their authority properly, and all three demonstrated respect for the authority of others.

- These women of God demonstrated holy boldness.

- Lives were saved because of their actions.

What did I learn from this chapter?

_____

_____

_____

_____

_____

_____

_____

_____

_____

_____

_____

_____

_____

_____

How?

How can I be a *chayil* woman? How can I encourage my husband to pursue the regal qualities described in Proverbs 31? Are these characteristics achievable? Can I really make a difference in my family, vocation, and the marketplace? Is it possible for my ministry to make a significant impact on society?

We can do all things through the power of Christ. We can achieve our greatest goals, from the least to the greatest, with His guidance and power (Philippians 4.13; Ephesians 3.20). God is concerned about every area of our lives and wants us to maximize each of them. However, He won't force us to be successful. Victory won't supernaturally drop into our laps. God did not physically fight Israel's battles but provided the strategy for their victory. God didn't come from heaven to save Esther's people but used her and her husband. The Shunammite woman had to leave home and track down Elisha to resolve her crisis. King Lemuel had to follow his mother's instructions to rule successfully and find his wife. God won't do the required work, but He will provide the necessary tools.

Study and execute the following Scriptures and principles. Allow God to empower you to make what seems impossible conceivable in your life. *"For with God nothing is or ever shall be impossible"* (Luke 1.37 AMP).

- Receive Jesus Christ as Lord and Savior. If Jesus isn't Lord of your life, He doesn't have your permission to mold you into the incredible person He predestined you to be. Salvation is for everyone who will have faith in the redemptive death, burial, and resurrection of Jesus. He died in your place on Calvary to give you abundant life on earth and eternal life after death. Jesus made provisions for you to have the best of now and forever. Receiving salvation requires repentance. Repentance is the willful act of turning away from anything that draws you away from Christ and embracing everything that will promote a strong relationship with Him. Although Jesus sacrificed His life for everyone, He won't force Himself upon anyone. Each individual must intentionally decide to be in covenant with Him (Matthew 16.25-26; John 3.16-17).

- Water baptism is thoroughly documented in the New Testament. It is the symbolic act that represents the washing away of our sins after repentance. Is it important? Yes. Jesus, who never sinned, submitted Himself to water baptism by John as an example for mankind. The book of Acts, which chronicles the beginnings of the New Testament Church (of which we who are saved are a part), documents the water baptisms of many. Some were immediately baptized at their times of repentance, yet others were water-baptized after being filled with the Holy Spirit. In a nutshell, everyone should be baptized in water (Matthew 3.13-17; Mark 16.16; The book of Acts).

- Every Christian needs the baptism of the Holy Ghost/ Spirit. Jesus told Nicodemus to be born again, he had to be born of water and Spirit. On the Day of Pentecost, all the followers of Christ in the upper room were filled with the Holy Ghost and spoke in "other tongues (languages)." There were no exceptions. Those in attendance included Mary, the mother of Jesus, and all of Jesus' hand-picked apostles (except Judas, who was dead). Since those who knew Jesus best needed to be baptized in the Spirit, none of us can deny our need. Some purposes of the baptism of the Holy Ghost are to empower us to be effective witness-

es, for personal spiritual edification, to make us spiritually equipped to overcome every evil power, and to position
us to receive and demonstrate the Gifts of the Spirit. All
you need to do is ask, then yield yourself to receive this
beautiful and life-changing experience (John 3.1-7; Acts
1.5, 8, 13-14; 2.1-18, 38; 19.1-6; 1 Corinthians 12.4-
11,14.2, 4).

- If you have not consistently striven to be all God has
  intended, you have cheated yourself. Why merely exist
  when you can thrive? Daily, give Jesus an authentic and
  fresh "yes" (Matthew 6.33; Mark 8.34; 2 Corinthians
  7.10; 3 John 1.2).

- Daily pursue the mind of Christ. Seek His wisdom, knowledge, and understanding through prayer and Bible study.
  Words are products of the mind. The Bible is "a small por-
  tion" of God's mind in print. You can't know Him without
  knowing His mind. Ask Jesus to give you an appetite for
  prayer and studying. Also, make it a daily practice to give
  God some of your "prime time," not your leftover time.
  Pray and study when you're at your mental peak. Cultivate the type of closeness with Jesus that fosters genuine
  communion. Relinquish your will and replace it with His
  (Psalm 119.11; Proverbs 16.16; Colossians 3.16; James
  1.5).

- Ask for assistance when needed. Deborah needed Barak.
  Esther needed Mordecai and her husband. The Shunammite woman needed Elisha. From time to time, everyone
  needs help to fulfill their assignments and deal with the
  issues of life. Be prayerful regarding who you ask. You
  want to be certain that the people you ask have your best
  interest at heart so they won't try to sabotage your mission
  or make things worse. Your helpers may be other wom-

en. Remember, you're not competitors but collaborators. In addition, be willing to lend a helping hand to others. Helping others achieve their goals shouldn't diminish yours. Remember the principle of sowing and reaping. You cannot refuse to be helpful yet expect help in your time of need.

- Don't be afraid! Changing old habits is uncomfortable. Walking in new territory can be a bit scary. Pray and obey at each juncture of the process. Don't doubt who you are, nor who you are becoming. Jesus will not ask you to do anything you're incapable of. But He will sometimes ask you to do things you may not want to do. Follow those Holy Ghost-inspired urges, even when you can't discern the outcome. Obey Him even when you don't understand Him. We don't walk by understanding but by faith! Do the work. Prepare for success (Proverbs 3.5-6; Isaiah 41.10; 2 Corinthians 5.7).

- Avoid blind visionaries. Stay away from lazy and apathetic people. Just as you wouldn't take health and fitness advice from someone who is 70 pounds overweight, don't take spiritual advice from someone who is spiritually unhealthy. Don't take relationship advice from someone who has never had a healthy relationship. Be leery of those who haven't accomplished their goals but want to tell you how to master yours. People without children may know some things about child-rearing, but remember that their knowledge is not experiential. Those who doubt your destiny don't need to know its details. Those who envy you now will do so even more as Jesus blesses you. Love them, but don't confide in them (Proverbs 20.19, Ecclesiastes 10.11).

- Continually pray for your relationships, family, ministry, vocation, and business endeavors. Real success is a process, not an event. It must be cultivated and nurtured for the duration of your life. It requires dedication, perseverance, and consistency. Prayerlessness results in failure, but prayerfulness results in fulfillment. Pray...obey...expect! (Luke 18.1; I Thessalonians 5.17)

What did I learn from this chapter?

_____

_____

_____

_____

_____

_____

_____

_____

_____

_____

_____

_____

_____

Concluding Prayer

Dear Jesus, I honor You. I praise and glorify You for all that has been revealed and confirmed in this book.

More than ever, I realize that You have wonderful things planned for my life. I know You are concerned about every detail of my life: every relationship, every educational pursuit, every business venture—*everything!* I believe You have already provided the tools, strategies, and people to help me attain and maintain the success ordained for me. I acknowledge that my happiness and wholeness can't be found in material possessions but only in You. My sense of stability and contentment comes through believing Your Word and resting in the peace of the Holy Spirit.

Lord, I repent for doubting my worth. Because I didn't see myself through Your eyes, I have also failed to see others from Your perspective. I repent for neglecting my responsibilities. I repent for my slothfulness and indifference. I repent for allowing myself to be distracted by the cares and entrapments of this world. I also repent for looking to the world for my role models. These things have caused me to waste valuable time and resources and make many unnecessary mistakes.

But now, my eyes are on You. The foundation of my perspective is from the Bible. Because I know better, I can now do better. Mediocrity is not acceptable. My outlook has changed. My life is properly prioritized. I surrender to Your plans. I don't want You to merely touch my life but transform it! Now, I am ready to confidently and graciously show the world genuine womanhood.

Regardless of where I began, I **will** finish strong. I **will** maximize my potential. I **will** accomplish every goal and fulfill every assignment. Many have seen me at my worst, but now they **will** see me at my best.

As I do these things, I **will** mindfully give You all the praise, honor, and glory. I seal this prayer in Your name, Lord Jesus... Amen!

Resources

Reed, Augusta M., ***GOD'S LADY, THE COMPLETE WOMAN***, Copyright 1995 by Augusta M. Reed. Used by permission. All rights reserved.

Reed, Augusta M., *IT'S NOT PUNISHMENT, IT'S PREPARATION*, Copyright 2013 by Augusta M. Reed. Used by permission. All rights reserved.

https://www.Merriam-Webster.com/dictionary/redeem, (accessed September 26, 2023). Used by permission. All Rights Reserved.

New World Encyclopedia contributors, "Ruby," New World Encyclopedia, https://www.newworldencyclopedia.org/p/index.php?title=Ruby&oldid=1108839, (accessed September 25, 2023). Used by permission. All Rights Reserved.

https://understandingthebible.org/how-old-was-esther-when-she-became-queen, (accessed November 1, 2023). Used by permission. All Rights Reserved.

https://en.wikipedia.org/wiki/Ruby, (accessed September 26, 2023). Used by permission. All Rights Reserved.
https://en.wikipedia.org/wiki/inclusion_(mineral), (accessed September 26, 2023. Used by permission. All Rights Reserved.

Help Others Find This Book!

- Post a picture on your social media accounts and share why you enjoyed it.

- Post a review on the online bookseller from which it was purchased.

- Encourage friends, family, and women's groups to purchase it.

- Give the book as a gift to someone you believe can benefit from it.

Thanks for Reading!

About the Author

Augusta M. (Hunter) Reed was born and raised in Cincinnati, Ohio. Augusta credits her parents, Doshie and Willie Hunter, as the two most influential persons who pointed her to Christ and encouraged her to be a woman of excellence and integrity.

At age 18, Augusta surrendered her life to Jesus Christ and immediately began to serve wherever she could. No opportunity was too small or menial. One of her personal mottos is, "If you're too important for a small task, you're too small for an important task." Over the past 52 years, her Kingdom service has included outreach ministry volunteer, Christian Education director, associate pastor, and lay counselor. She continues to travel throughout the country, speaking for conferences and retreats. In recent years, a significant emphasis of her ministry has been serving widowed women and men. Her passion and compassion for the grieving stems from her own personal losses, including the passing of her husband, Clarence, in 1999.

Augusta is a retired Speech-Language Pathologist and professional mentor. She often says Jesus cleverly led her into ministry through her profession. In addition to her professional credentials, Augusta has completed extensive training in Biblical Studies, Christian counseling, and life coaching.

Augusta currently lives in Ohio. She is the mother of Jayson and Candace and grandmother of Noah.

Contact Augusta

- Elderaugusta@gmail.com

- Facebook.com/augusta.reed

- Instagram:@ladyaugusta66

Other Books by Augusta M. Reed

(available on Amazon.com)

It's Not Punishment, It's Preparation

Pearls For All Occasions

Without Pain

From Sorrow to Joy: Paths to Restoration for Remaining Spouses

www.ingramcontent.com/pod-product-compliance
Lightning Source LLC
Chambersburg PA
CBHW070028030426
42335CB00017B/2337